**OVERCOMING ADVERSITY:**
SHARING THE AMERICAN DREAM

# BARACK OBAMA

**CAMMY S. BOURCIER**

MASON CREST PUBLISHERS
PHILADELPHIA

# ABOUT CROSS-CURRENTS

When you see this logo, turn to the Cross-Currents section at the back of the book. The Cross-Currents features explore connections between people, places, events, and ideas.

Produced by OTTN Publishing, Stockton, New Jersey

**Mason Crest Publishers**
370 Reed Road
Broomall, PA 19008
www.masoncrest.com

3 5 7 9 8 6 4 2

Library of Congress Cataloging-in-Publication Data

Bourcier, Cammy S.
  Barack Obama / Cammy S. Bourcier.
      p. cm. — (Sharing the american dream)
  Includes bibliographical references.
  ISBN 978-1-4222-0574-7 (hardcover) — ISBN 978-1-4222-0759-8 (pbk.)
  1. Obama, Barack—Juvenile literature. 2. Presidential candidates—United
States—Biography—Juvenile literature. 3. Legislators—United
States—Biography—Juvenile literature. 4. African American
legislators—Biography—Juvenile literature. 5. United States. Congress.
Senate—Biography—Juvenile literature. 6. African Americans—Biography—Juvenile litera-
ture. 7. Racially mixed people—United States—Biography--Juvenile literature. I. Title.
  E901.1.023B68 2008
  328.73092—dc22
  [B]
                                          2008024460

OVERCOMING ADVERSITY:
SHARING THE AMERICAN DREAM

# TABLE OF CONTENTS

# CHAPTER ONE

# A VOICE FOR UNITY

On March 18, 2008, Senator Barack Obama stood at a podium in the National Constitution Center in Philadelphia. He had come to this place—just two blocks from where the Declaration of Independence was signed in 1776—to deliver a speech about one of the most difficult, painful, and controversial subjects in American life: race.

## A Political Firestorm

Barack Obama could bring an unusual perspective to the issue of race. His father was black and his mother white. He was raised largely by his white grandparents but, because of his skin color, was always identified as an African American by people who didn't know him. On occasion, he experienced white bigotry firsthand. Yet when he first ran for Congress in a largely African American district in Chicago, he also faced charges that he wasn't "black enough."

By 2008 Obama's 12-year political career had taken him from the Illinois statehouse to the U.S. Senate to a run for president of the United States. Political analysts considered him the first African American candidate with a real chance of winning the presidency. In large measure, the commentators said, that

OVERCOMING ADVERSITY:
SHARING THE AMERICAN DREAM

# BARACK OBAMA

MASON CREST PUBLISHERS
PHILADELPHIA

OVERCOMING ADVERSITY:
SHARING THE AMERICAN DREAM

Senator Barack Obama, Democratic candidate for president, speaks at the National Constitution Center in Philadelphia, March 18, 2008. His subject was race.

was because Obama was a "post-racial" figure. He was black, but that wasn't central to his political identity. He didn't frame issues in racial terms, the way other prominent African American leaders, such as the Reverend Jesse Jackson and the Reverend Al Sharpton, often did. And he wasn't divisive. He could appeal to white as well as black voters.

In March 2008, however, Obama was pulled into a firestorm of racially charged controversy. It erupted after TV news organizations and Internet sites began playing a short clip from an old sermon by Obama's longtime friend and former pastor, the Reverend Jeremiah Wright. On April 13, 2003, Wright had delivered a sermon titled "Confusing God and Government" at Trinity United Church of Christ in Chicago. The United States had recently invaded Iraq, and Wright criticized President George W. Bush and his supporters for implying that the war was somehow carrying out God's will. Governments, Wright said, often lie and fail to carry out the will of God. Many of the examples he used to illustrate this point concerned ways the U.S. government had mistreated people of color, including taking the land of American Indians and enslaving black people. He also claimed that the government had created the virus that causes AIDS to wipe out people of color. For these and other offenses, Wright said, God would not bless America but damn it.

The Reverend Jeremiah Wright Jr., whose fiery sermons created controversy during the 2008 presidential campaign.

As the clip of Wright shouting "God damn America!" was replayed endlessly, critics accused the pastor of being unpatriotic. They also said he was a racist.

The controversy threatened to derail Barack Obama's campaign for the presidency. Although Obama had rejected his former pastor's most inflammatory comments, people were demanding to know how the senator could have remained a member of Wright's congregation for 20 years.

Discussions of race in America can quickly explode into angry finger pointing between blacks and whites. Perhaps that is why many Americans—and especially politicians—prefer to avoid speaking directly and candidly about the issue. As the controversy surrounding Jeremiah Wright swirled, however, Barack Obama decided that he didn't have that luxury.

## Speaking of Race

Obama began his March 18 speech by echoing the first words of the Constitution of the United States: "We the people, in order to form a more perfect union." He noted that, when America's Founding Fathers produced it in 1787, the Constitution was unfinished because it permitted slavery to continue. But generations of Americans had worked to help perfect the union by ending slavery and winning equal rights for all citizens. And one of the goals of his presidential campaign, Obama said, was "to continue the long march of those who came before us, a march for a more just, more equal, more free, more caring and more prosperous America."

**READ MORE**

The U.S. Constitution, drafted in 1787, failed to bring the blessings of liberty to America's slaves. The country has suffered a troubled racial legacy since that time. For a brief overview, see page 46.

Obama said that Reverend Wright's racially charged comments had divided America at a time when the country needed unity in order to confront its many pressing problems. But even if he considered some of Wright's views wrong, Obama refused to reject the minister, noting that Wright was like family to him. "I can no more disown him," Obama declared, "than I can disown the black community. I can no more disown him than I can my white grandmother—a woman who helped raise me . . . a woman who loves me as much as she loves anything in this world, but a woman who once confessed her fear of black men who passed by her on the street, and who on more than one occasion has uttered racial or ethnic stereotypes that made me cringe."

Reverend Wright's anger at America's history of mistreating blacks, Obama maintained, had led the minister to a distorted and stereotyped view of the nation. Wright's mistake, he went on to say, was not in condemning racism. Rather, his mistake was in failing to recognize that America could change—and in fact had changed—for the better.

Yet Obama insisted that this is no reason for complacency. Anger in the African American community persists, he said, because the legacy of discrimination continues to blight the lives of many black people—in ways such as reduced educational achievement, intense poverty in urban areas, and high levels of violence. At the same time, Obama said, anger exists among many whites, who believe that because they are not personally responsible for past injustices against African Americans, they shouldn't be made to pay for those injustices by, for example, having to bus their children to an inner-city school or having to give up a spot at the college of their choice in favor of a black student with lower test scores.

This racial stalemate, Obama said, wouldn't be easily broken. But he expressed his "firm conviction—a conviction rooted in my faith in God and my faith in the American people—that working together we can move beyond some of our old racial wounds, and that in fact we have no choice if we are to continue on the path of a more perfect union." He urged African Americans to keep insisting on a full measure of justice in every sphere of American society, but at the same time to take responsibility for their own lives. In addition, Obama said, blacks should recognize that Americans of all backgrounds share such concerns as having decent health care, good schools for their children, and good jobs. Whites, for their part, must recognize that discrimination against African Americans continues—even if it is less obvious than in the past. Whites must commit themselves to eliminating discrimination by taking concrete actions such as investing in

With his message of unity and positive change, Barack Obama drew large, enthusiastic—and diverse—crowds all over the country during his presidential campaign. Seen here is an October 11, 2008, rally in Philadelphia.

education and insisting that civil rights laws are always enforced. Ultimately, Obama said, the path to a more perfect union requires all Americans to realize that their dreams don't have to come at the expense of the dreams of another person or group— that the entire country can prosper together. "Let us find that common stake we all have in one another," he urged.

## A Living Bridge?

Many observers judged Barack Obama's speech at the National Constitution Center to be extraordinary, even historic. "After running a campaign that in many ways tried not to be defined by race," reporter Jeff Zeleny wrote in the *New York Times*, "Mr. Obama placed himself squarely in the middle of the debate over how to address it, a living bridge between whites and blacks still divided by the legacy of slavery and all that came after it."

Writing for *U.S. News & World Report*, Liz Halloran quoted African American scholars who found in Obama's remarks "about slavery, black anger, white resentment, and the imperative to move forward" echoes of two of the most important figures in U.S. history: President Abraham Lincoln and civil rights leader Martin Luther King Jr. Whether Obama's contributions to the nation would one day justify that comparison remained to be seen.

# CHAPTER TWO

# FROM BARRY TO BARACK

Barack Hussein Obama was born in Honolulu, Hawaii, on August 4, 1961. His parents came from very different backgrounds. Barack Obama Sr., a member of the Luo tribe, grew up in a small rural village in the East African country of Kenya. As a child, he tended his father's goats. His intelligence eventually earned him a scholarship to study in the United States. He became the first African student to enroll at the University of Hawaii, where he studied economics. There he met Stanley Ann Dunham, a young anthropology student whose father had wanted a boy so badly he'd given her his first name. She had lived in Kansas, Texas, Oklahoma, and Washington State before moving with her parents to Hawaii right after graduating from high school.

Barack Obama with his mother, Ann, circa 1963.

Ann (she had since stopped using her unusual first name) was 18 when she and the 23-year-old Barack Obama had a Russian-language class together. They soon fell in love and decided to marry.

At first Ann's parents, Stan and Madelyn Dunham, weren't fond of the idea of their daughter marrying a black man. But they grew to like Barack

Kenyan-born Barack Obama Sr. was studying economics at the University of Hawaii when he met and married Ann Dunham.

Obama for his friendliness and keen intelligence. The story was completely different with Hussein Onyango Obama, who was furious when his son wrote from Hawaii to inform him of his marriage plans. Onyango objected to his son marrying a white woman—and besides, Barack Obama Sr. already had a wife and two children in his home village in Kenya. In spite of this, Ann and Barack went ahead and got married.

But they would not remain together for long. In 1963, two years after the birth of their son, Barack—whom they called Barry— the elder Barack Obama graduated from the University of Hawaii. He had two scholarship offers to pursue a Ph.D. One, from the New School of Social Research in New York City, included money for living expenses, which would allow Ann and young Barry to go with him. The other, from Harvard University in Cambridge, Massachusetts, did not. Barack Obama chose Harvard, believing it to be a more distinguished school.

This decision strained the marriage of Barry's parents past the breaking point. They divorced in 1964. Barry would grow up not knowing his father, whom he would see again only once in his life, at the age of 10.

Ann, meanwhile, continued her education. She and young Barry lived with her parents.

# In Indonesia

As she worked toward her degree at the University of Hawaii, Ann Dunham met and fell in love with another foreign student, Lolo Soetoro. He was from Indonesia, an island nation in

Southeast Asia. In 1967, Lolo and Ann decided to get married. Lolo returned to Indonesia and built a home in a village on the outskirts of Jakarta, the capital city. Several months later Ann and six-year-old Barry joined him there.

Barry found life in Indonesia quite different from life in Hawaii. To begin, chickens and ducks roamed the yard of his new home, and in a fenced-off pond there were two alligators. Family pets included an ape, a cockatoo, and two birds of paradise.

Lolo insisted that his stepson learn where his dinner came from, so he showed Barry how to kill a chicken. Soon Barry was also eating more exotic foods, including dog meat, snake meat, and roasted grasshopper.

Barry began learning the Indonesian language and played with the local children. They rode water buffalo, trapped crickets, played soccer, and flew kites. He later recalled the time as "one long adventure, the bounty of a young boy's life." But there were also some disturbing aspects of life in Indonesia— including the grinding poverty, which could be seen in the

(Above) Barack Obama with his stepfather, mother, and half sister, Maya, in Indonesia. After the breakup of his mother's second marriage, he went to live with her parents in Hawaii. (Right) Barack and his grandparents Stanley and Madelyn Dunham at Barack's high school graduation, 1979.

large number of beggars and in the people with untreated illnesses and disfiguring conditions.

For first grade, Barry's mother and stepfather enrolled him in Fransiskus Assisi, a Catholic school that was near the family's house. He attended Fransiskus Assisi for two years. After Barry reached the third grade, Lolo landed a well-paying job, which enabled the family to move to a fashionable neighborhood in Jakarta. Barry was then sent to a public school, State Elementary School Besuki (now called SDN Menteng No. 1). It was considered one of the best schools in Jakarta.

Nevertheless, Ann Dunham worried about the education her son was receiving in Indonesia. Her marriage to Lolo Soetoro was also disintegrating. These factors contributed to Ann's decision to send Barry back to Hawaii in 1971, after he had finished fourth grade. He would live with his grandparents and attend school there. For the time being at least, Ann would remain in Indonesia with Lolo and Barry's half sister, Maya, who had been born in 1970.

## Identity Crisis

In the fall of 1971, Barry Obama started fifth grade at Punahou, one of the most prestigious schools in Hawaii. He had been awarded a scholarship. At first, he remembers, he felt very out of place. Most of his classmates had gone to school together since kindergarten, and he didn't know anybody. In addition, Punahou had few African Americans like him, and while many of the students came from wealthy families, his grandparents were of modest means.

Eventually, however, Barry seemed to adjust well to his new circumstances. He developed a group of close friends. He was a good student who read widely. In high school, he wrote for Punahou Academy's literary magazine. He also played on

(Top) The Punahou School, in Honolulu, Hawaii.
(Right) Barack's high school senior portrait.

Punahou's varsity basketball team, which won a state basketball championship. Classmates and teachers would recall him as sometimes quiet, but popular, good-natured, and seemingly at ease with himself.

Behind his cheerful façade, however, Barry Obama apparently struggled with difficult personal issues. He was, by his own later admission, an angry and conflicted teen who experimented with drugs to ease his emotional pain. Keith Kakugawa, a close friend from high school, told a reporter in 2007 that Obama's "biggest struggles were his feelings of abandonment" by his parents. Barry's father visited him just once, at Christmas time in 1971. His mother returned to Hawaii with Maya in 1973 but went back to live in Indonesia three years later.

In his 1995 memoir, *Dreams from My Father: A Story of Race and Inheritance*, Barack Obama revealed a different reason for his emotional turmoil: his inability to come to terms with his racial identity. Because he lived with his white grandparents (and, during the time she was in Hawaii, his white mother), he was in some respects part of the white world. But in America, his skin color would always mark him as black. People treated him differently, he believed, because they classified him as an African American, and this angered him deeply. He felt like an outsider, caught between two worlds. He yearned to belong fully to the African American community, but he really didn't know how he should act or what values he needed to embrace to do that. "I was," he wrote in *Dreams from My Father*, "engaged in a fitful interior struggle. I was trying to raise myself to be a black man in America, and beyond the given of my appearance, no one around me seemed to know what that meant."

## College Years

Despite his inner conflicts, Obama managed to graduate from Punahou with good grades. He was accepted into Occidental College, a small, private college in Los Angeles. He enrolled there in the fall of 1979.

The young man from Hawaii impressed his teachers at Occidental. "Clearly the guy had a presence," Eric L. Newhall, an English professor, recalled. "He came off as a serious, intelligent, articulate guy."

Outside the classroom, Barack Obama would say later, his political consciousness awakened. He became involved in demonstrations on Occidental's campus to protest apartheid, the policy by which South Africa's white majority kept its nonwhite majority oppressed. Obama also came to terms with who he was. "My identity might begin with the fact of my race," he wrote in *Dreams from My Father*, but it didn't, couldn't end there." The values that matter—justice, honesty, compassion, kindness—are neither black nor white. Community must be based on more than skin color alone.

Obama decided to devote himself to public policy. After his sophomore year at Occidental, he transferred to Columbia University in New York City to concentrate on his studies.

In New York, he made some changes in his personal life, becoming more disciplined. He ran several miles a day and fasted on Sundays. He also stopped calling himself Barry and began using his given name, Barack. He made plans to visit his father in Kenya. Unfortunately, that visit would never happen: in 1982 his half sister Auma called Obama to inform him that their father had died in a car accident.

In 1983, Obama graduated from Columbia University with a degree in political science. He planned to work fighting discrimination and poverty.

Obama takes a break from his studies at Columbia University to enjoy New York City's Central Park.

# CHAPTER THREE

# ROOTS OF A CAREER

During his final semester at Columbia University, Barack Obama had decided to become a community organizer, though he had only a vague idea about what that would actually involve. In New York, he had seen social conditions that bothered his conscience. In a city where some people lived in luxurious penthouses or brownstone mansions, others endured grinding poverty in their decaying neighborhoods. Obama believed that American society was in need of fundamental change. But he didn't expect that change to come from the government. Instead, Obama believed that society would have to be changed from the ground up.

Obama wrote to every group he thought might be able to use his services as a community organizer. He got no responses. So, forced to make a living, he took a position as a research assistant at a New York City company that did consulting work for corporations. Eventually, he was promoted to financial writer. He was making a good salary and had his own office and secre-

## READ MORE

For information about what community organizers do, and for a profile of the man known as the father of modern community organizing, see page 48.

tary. Still, he would recall later, he "felt pangs of guilt for my lack of resolve" in finding a job that would help poor people.

Around this time, Obama received a call from his half sister Auma, whom he had never met. She informed him that one of their brothers, David, had been killed in a motorcycle accident. Obama had never met David either, but the news left him vaguely unsettled. A few months later, he resigned from his job at the consulting firm and again began looking for a position as a community organizer.

## Finding a Job

Obama eventually took a job promoting recycling in New York City's Harlem neighborhood. He also briefly worked for a political campaign in Brooklyn, New York, passing out flyers. Within six months, he was unemployed and broke. And then, finally, came an opportunity.

Obama answered a help-wanted ad for a Chicago-based group called the Calumet Community Religious Conference (CCRC). Headed by veteran community organizer Gerald Kellman, the group was trying to halt the neighborhood decay that afflicted Chicago's South Side and the city's southern suburbs. Hard times had befallen these

Those who have worked closely with Barack Obama—from his years as a community organizer in Chicago to his run for president of the United States—describe him as principled yet practical.

areas when manufacturing industries, especially steel mills, had closed. The CCRC hoped to attract jobs and to help residents obtain the municipal services they needed and deserved.

One of the basic principles of community organizing is that there is power in numbers. The more people there are acting together, the greater the likelihood officials will respond to their demands. Kellman wanted to get urban and suburban residents to band together. But he had a problem: he and his organizing partners were white, and while they were making inroads in the predominantly white suburbs, they had failed to gain the trust of residents of Chicago's predominantly black South Side. Kellman was looking for an African American organizer to work with the black churches of the South Side. On a trip to New York City he interviewed Obama at a coffeehouse. After a few minutes, he offered Obama the job. Despite the low salary, Obama accepted.

## South Side Organizer

In June 1985, Barack Obama arrived in Chicago. He was not yet 24 and had no experience as a community organizer. Despite this, people with whom Obama worked would recall him as extraordinarily confident. "The guy was just totally comfortable with who he was and where he was," colleague John Owens remembered more than 20 years later. For his part, Gerald Kellman was impressed by the drive his young organizer exhibited. "He was ambitious," Kellman said of Obama, "but never just for ambition's sake. It was always mixed in with a sense of service."

Obama spent much of his time working with residents of Altgeld Gardens, a large housing project on the South Side. Built some 40 years earlier, Altgeld Gardens was in disrepair. Many of its 2,000 units had crumbling plaster, leaky roofs, plumbing that frequently backed up, and an unreliable heating system.

Apartment units of Altgeld Gardens, a huge housing project on Chicago's South Side. Barack Obama tried to organize Altgeld residents to improve their living conditions.

Obama mobilized Altgeld residents. He helped them take their grievances to the Chicago Housing Authority (CHA), which ran Altgeld. CHA officials weren't quick to respond, but Obama and the residents kept up the pressure. Some repairs were made.

In the meantime, Obama found another issue to address. The Illinois state legislature had established a computerized job bank to help unemployed workers in Chicago find jobs. There were job-placement offices throughout the city, but none within 35 blocks of Altgeld Gardens—even though unemployment in the projects was very high. Obama organized residents to change this situation. They held rallies and petitioned Mayor Harold Washington. Eventually, the mayor agreed to locate a job-placement office near Altgeld.

# Religious Matters

In much of his organizing work, Obama sought to enlist the support of South Side pastors. The black churches played a key role in people's lives, and they had a lot of political power. Unfortunately, the pastors often competed for congregants and were jealous of one

A parishioner exits Trinity United Church of Christ.

another's influence. This was one reason Obama found it difficult to get the pastors to work together. But there was another reason, a pastor told Obama one day. The church leaders all knew that Obama himself didn't attend church. Maybe they would trust him more, the pastor suggested, if Obama joined a congregation.

Obama had not had a religious upbringing. During his years in Indonesia, he had received some instruction at school in the Catholic and Muslim faiths. But this hadn't made much of an impression, he would later say. His mother was a nonbeliever; his grandparents had been Protestants but by the time they raised him had stopped going to church.

Obama decided to heed the advice of the Chicago pastor, however. He began attending services at Trinity United Church of Christ, which was led by the Reverend Jeremiah Wright. Obama would find a spiritual home at Trinity, and over the years Wright would become his religious mentor and friend.

## The Limits of Community Organizing

Barack Obama spent nearly three years as a community organizer in Chicago. He saw many real, if limited, successes. But he also saw constant setbacks. For example, Obama helped Altgeld residents force the Chicago Housing Authority to remove asbestos (an insulating material that can cause lung cancer) from their apartments. But the cost of doing this meant that the CHA couldn't make other needed repairs, such as fixing leaky roofs and substandard plumbing. Obama also found it difficult to keep residents unified and mobilized to improve their lives. Residents squabbled among themselves. Many complained that they were too busy simply trying to make ends meet to devote time to public action.

By 1987 Obama had confessed his frustrations to Gerald Kellman. He spoke of finding a more effective way of helping poor people. The sudden death of Harold Washington, Chicago's first black mayor, apparently helped crystallize Obama's thinking. Through his political career, Washington had done much to help Chicago's neediest citizens, especially in the African American community, and a law degree was what had enabled Washington to enter politics in the first place. "I just can't get things done here without a law degree," Obama told a good friend.

Obama applied for admission to Harvard Law School. In February 1988 he received notification that he had been accepted. Obama resigned his position with the CCRC in May, and over the summer he traveled to Kenya, his father's homeland. There he met many of his relatives.

# Harvard Law

In the fall of 1988, when he entered Harvard Law School, Barack Obama stood apart from his classmates in several ways. At 27, he was older than most of his fellow first-year law students. And, perhaps because of his unusual background and his three years as a community organizer, he appeared to have a broader perspective than most. He had a great ability to understand competing arguments, and he always seemed respectful of other people's points of view. "A lot of people at the time were just talking past each other," recalled Harvard classmate Crystal Nix Hines, "very committed to their opinions, their point of view, and not particularly interested in what other people had to say. Barack transcended that."

In addition to his open manner, Obama impressed his class-mates and professors with his intellectual brilliance. Professor Laurence Tribe, a leading constitutional scholar, called Obama "one of the two most talented students I've had in 37 years in teaching."

Obama also studied diligently, and by the end of his first year he ranked near the top of his class. This made him eligible for a position as an editor of the student-run *Harvard Law Review*. Arguably the most prestigious legal journal in the country, it publishes articles by professors, legal scholars, judges, and other leading figures in the field of law. Obama secured his position on the *Harvard Law Review* by submitting an outstanding essay.

During his second year at Harvard, Obama decided to run for president of the *Law Review*. For some time, politics had paralyzed the *Law Review* staff. One of the most divisive issues was affirmative action. Liberals on the staff thought Harvard—and American society in general—should do more to guarantee positions of importance to African Americans, women, and members of other historically disadvantaged groups. Conservatives blasted this as reverse discrimination. Obama confided to several friends that he believed he could dampen the hostility on the *Law Review* staff and get everyone working together.

The election for *Law Review* president was held on February 5, 1990. There were 19 candidates. Each was critically examined by the more than 60 remaining

Barack Obama, president of the *Harvard Law Review*, with members of his staff, 1990.

editors. Periodically, ballots would be cast and a few candidates would be eliminated. Many hours into the process, after the last conservative had been eliminated and only a few candidates were left, the conservatives threw their support to Barack Obama, ensuring him victory. "Whatever his politics, we felt he would give us a fair shake," recalled Bradford Berenson, a member of the conservative faction.

As the first African American president in the 100-year history of the *Harvard Law Review*, Barack Obama became a minor celebrity. Newspaper reporters interviewed him. A publisher commissioned him to write a book; it would appear in 1995 as *Dreams from My Father*.

By all accounts, Obama's tenure as president of the *Law Review* was very successful. He managed to defuse the tensions between liberals and conservatives. Though himself liberal, Obama appointed conservative editors to positions of authority. His leadership style was naturally inclusive, and conservative editors believed he gave their views a fair hearing. Obama also managed to avoid the pitfalls of racial politics. To the disappointment of some black students at Harvard, he didn't use his position to advance a specifically African American agenda. Instead, according to members of his staff, he encouraged blacks and whites to work together, emphasized consensus, and sought always to create a high-quality publication. "This bridge-building approach to racial and partisan politics was the first indication of the tightrope he would walk through his career," Obama biographer David Mendell later wrote.

In 1991 Obama received a JD (doctor of laws) degree from Harvard, graduating with honors. In a speech that spring to the Black Law Students Association, Obama had urged his peers to use their degrees not simply to make a lot of money, but to help less privileged members of society.

# CHAPTER FOUR

# LEGISLATING FOR CHANGE

After graduating from Harvard Law School in 1991, Barack Obama returned to Chicago. His plan had always been to resume advocating for the city's underprivileged African American communities after getting a law degree. But now there were also personal reasons to go back to Chicago. He was in love.

Obama had met Michelle Robinson after his first year in law school. He was doing a summer internship at the Chicago law firm where she worked, and she was his supervisor. Herself a graduate of Harvard Law School, Michelle had grown up on Chicago's South Side in a very closely knit, working-class family. The two began to date, and by the time Obama returned to Chicago in 1991, they were engaged to be married. The wedding took place in October 1992, at Trinity United Church of Christ, with the Reverend Jeremiah Wright presiding.

Barack and Michelle Obama on their wedding day, October 18, 1992.

Obama had been very busy since graduating from Harvard. He'd worked on his memoir, which would take several more years to finish. He'd also taken a job as director of Illinois Project Vote, a voter-registration campaign that sought to bring low-income minorities into the political process.

In 1993 Obama took a job at a small Chicago law firm specializing in civil rights law. He also began teaching law at the University of Chicago Law School.

# Entering Politics

Obama had been thinking about seeking public office for some time when he got what seemed to be an ideal opportunity. In 1995 Alice Palmer, an African American state senator from the 13th District on Chicago's South Side, decided to give up her seat in the Illinois legislature in order to run for U.S. Congress. Palmer, a Democrat, was very popular, and she endorsed Obama to fill her state senate seat in the heavily Democratic 13th District. In July 1995 Obama launched his campaign.

In November of that year, however, Palmer lost in her race for the U.S. Congress. She soon changed her mind about vacating her state senate seat. Palmer's supporters, who included some of Chicago's most influential Democrats, pressured Obama to end his campaign. He refused, even though doing so would have gained him powerful allies for any future run for office. But Obama believed he was already connecting with voters. "People are hungry for community," he told the *Chicago Reader*, in a message that would figure prominently in his later political career. "They are hungry for change."

Meanwhile, Palmer's supporters scrambled to beat a December 18 deadline for gathering enough voter signatures to get her name placed on the Democratic primary ballot. They believed they had succeeded. But in January, Obama had a legal team challenge the validity of many signatures on Palmer's nominating petitions. Enough were found to be forged or improperly gathered that Palmer fell short of the required number.

Obama ran unopposed in the March 1996 Democratic primary. In November he easily beat his Republican opponent in the general election.

## State Senator

In January 1997, at the age of 36, Barack Obama began his career as a legislator. He soon found out that addressing the issues he believed were important wouldn't be easy. Republicans dominated both houses of the General Assembly of Illinois, and therefore they controlled the legislative agenda. As a Democrat, Obama would have limited influence. As a newcomer, he would have less influence still. And many of his Democratic colleagues in the state senate resented the way Obama had unseated the popular Alice Palmer.

Obama's instincts were to build bridges, as he had done at the *Harvard Law Review*. Obama sought out senate minority leader Emil Jones, who had been a Palmer supporter. He told Jones that he wanted to work with him, and Jones responded by giving the freshman lawmaker important assignments. These included crafting an ethics reform bill and working with Republicans to hammer out a welfare reform package. Obama gradually won the respect of his Republican colleagues through his thoughtful, methodical approach; his respectful tone; and his willingness to compromise while staying true to his principles.

"He is idealistic but practical . . . he has good attention to ideals and core principles," said John Bouman, a director of Chicago's National Center for Poverty Law. "But he recognizes that it is good to get things done from year to year. He is willing

Illinois state senate president Emil Jones speaks during the 2008 Democratic National Convention. Jones has been a longtime Obama supporter.

to hammer out a good compromise, but he doesn't compromise for the sake of it."

By 1999 Obama was regarded as a rising star in the Illinois Democratic Party. He decided to run for a seat in the U.S. House of Representatives in 2000. But he was soundly defeated by four-term congressman Bobby Rush.

After his electoral loss to Bobby Rush, Obama returned to the Illinois state senate. He pushed hard for legislation to help the poor and disadvantaged. He championed tax credits for the working poor. He voted to raise the state minimum wage. Obama won Republican support for legislation overhauling capital punishment in Illinois. This legislation was designed to prevent

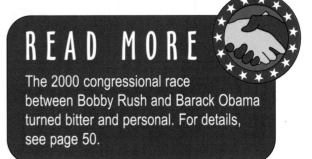

READ MORE

The 2000 congressional race between Bobby Rush and Barack Obama turned bitter and personal. For details, see page 50.

the execution of innocent defendants as well as to ensure that the death penalty was applied fairly, without regard to race or class. Obama also wrote a bill that expanded coverage, under the state's health insurance system, to 20,000 more children, and he offered a proposal to provide all children with health insurance.

In June 2001 the Obamas welcomed their second child, a daughter named Sasha. Sasha's older sister, Malia, had been born in 1998. Michelle insisted that Barack help raise the children, and he would later say that he wondered whether he had time to fulfill both his duties as a father and his responsibilities as a legislator. In the end, however, he decided to stand for reelection in 2002. He ran unopposed.

Michelle Obama with daughters Sasha (left) and Malia (right).

But even before voters had officially given Obama their approval for a second term in the Illinois state senate, he had turned his attention to national affairs. The United States appeared headed for a war that Obama believed would be a mistake.

# Taking a Stand

On September 11, 2001, Muslim terrorists belonging to the group al-Qaeda had hijacked four commercial airliners and attacked New York and Washington, D.C., killing about 3,000 Americans. Al-Qaeda's leaders were based in Afghanistan, where they were sheltered by that country's extremist Islamic government, the Taliban. When the Taliban refused to hand over al-Qaeda's leaders to face justice, U.S. president George W. Bush ordered an invasion of Afghanistan in October 2001. The Taliban was quickly overthrown, and al-Qaeda scattered.

Almost immediately, however, the Bush administration began planning for another war—this one to overthrow the regime of dictator Saddam Hussein in Iraq. The administration put forward several reasons for invading Iraq: that Saddam had worked with al-Qaeda; that he had stockpiles of banned "weapons of mass destruction" (nuclear, chemical, and biological weapons); that he presented a "grave and gathering threat" to the United States. All of these rationales for war would later be discredited, but by the fall of 2002 most Americans supported an invasion.

Barack Obama did not. At an antiwar rally in Chicago on October 2, 2002, Obama spoke forcefully against the Bush administration's plans. Obama noted that while he wasn't against all wars—some, he conceded, are necessary—he did oppose this war, which he said was "based not on reason but on passion, not on principle but on politics." Obama also doubted the Bush administration's rosy predictions of a quick and easy victory in Iraq.

## Onto the National Stage

In January 2003, Barack Obama announced his intention to seek the Democratic nomination for the U.S. Senate seat held by Republican Peter Fitzgerald. In April, Fitzgerald declared that he wouldn't run for reelection. Soon the Democratic field was crowded with candidates.

To win in a statewide race, Obama would have to appeal to a much more diverse electorate than he represented in the state senate. His 13th District on Chicago's South Side was predominantly African American. But now Obama would also have to win support in areas that were largely white, rural, and agricultural. In a speech in Chicago, Obama made it clear that he considered race a non-issue. "I am not running a race-based campaign," he said. "I am rooted in the African-American community but not limited by it." At a rally in rural Illinois, Obama told voters, "We have shared values—values that aren't black or white or Hispanic—values that are American, and Democratic."

In March 2004, Obama won the Democratic nomination by a wide margin. But his path to Congress still appeared difficult. The Republican nominee, Jack Ryan, was also an impressive candidate. Ryan was a multimillionaire businessman who, like Obama, had graduated from Harvard Law School. In June, however, Ryan withdrew from the race after embarrassing allegations made by his former wife became public. The Republican Party scrambled to find a replacement candidate.

Meanwhile, Barack Obama got a huge boost when the Democratic Party's presidential nominee, John Kerry, invited him to deliver the keynote address at the Democratic National

Obama gives the keynote address at the 2004 Democratic National Convention in Boston, Massachusetts.

Convention in Boston. On July 27, Obama gave a speech titled "The Audacity of Hope." In it he described his unusual background—with his black Kenyan father and his white Kansan mother and grandparents—and spoke of America's promise. The speech electrified listeners. It was widely judged to rank among the best keynote addresses ever delivered at an American political convention.

By early August, the Republicans had found a candidate to run against Obama—Alan Keyes, a prominent black conservative and former presidential candidate. Keyes never had a chance. In November, Obama won a stunning 70 percent of the vote.

Overall, however, the Democratic Party had little to cheer about. Kerry lost to the incumbent president, George W. Bush, and the Republicans picked up seats in both chambers of Congress. Some disheartened Democrats looked to Obama to change their party's fortunes—before he had even served a day in the U.S. Senate.

# CHAPTER FIVE

# ROAD TO THE WHITE HOUSE

Barack Obama took the oath of office as a U.S. senator on January 4, 2005. The event received an unusual amount of media attention. Obama was the only African American in the U.S. Senate—and just the third to serve in that body since 1877. Moreover, his dynamic speech at the Democratic National Convention, along with his fascinating personal history, had made him something of a celebrity. Obama's early opposition to the war in Iraq also set him apart from the vast majority of members of Congress (including leading Democrats), who had voted in 2002 to authorize the use of force in Iraq. By 2005, as the fighting raged on and U.S. casualties mounted, an increasing number of Americans were beginning to believe the invasion had been a mistake, as Obama had warned. Many people had great expectations for the freshman senator.

## Rookie Senator

Obama tried to play down those expectations. Democrats were the minority party in the U.S. Senate. Plus, it would take time for him to learn how the Senate operated. "I'm feeling very much like the rookie," he said, "and looking for guidance from those who've been [in the Senate] for 15 or 20 years."

One of those senior senators was Illinois Democrat Dick Durbin, with whom Obama collaborated on veterans' issues. Another was Republican Richard Lugar of Indiana, an expert on international affairs. Lugar and Obama worked together on legislation designed to keep terrorists from acquiring nuclear weapons as well as certain kinds of advanced conventional weapons, such as shoulder-fired missiles.

In early 2006, Obama helped write ethics and lobbying reform legislation; it became law the following year. Overall, however, Obama's legislative accomplishments during his first year and a half in the Senate were modest. This isn't surprising, as the Senate operates largely on seniority.

Obama continued to maintain a high public profile throughout 2006, however. He drew enthusiastic crowds on a national book tour to promote his newly published *The Audacity of Hope*, which became a bestseller. He was also well received as he crisscrossed the country campaigning for Democratic congressional candidates.

On Election Day in November, the Democrats made big gains, retaking control of the Senate and House of Representatives. Political analysts suggested that the results reflected Americans' disillusionment with the war in Iraq and anger at the Republican Party over a series of scandals.

With the mood of the country favoring his party, and with his personal popularity at a high point, Barack Obama began seriously considering a run for president of the United States in 2008. However, he worried that, with only two years in the Senate under his belt, voters might see him as too inexperienced for the nation's highest office. Obama sought counsel from close advisers and colleagues such as Senator Dick Durbin. Durbin told him that he might never have a better opportunity.

Obama and senator Dick Durbin at a 2005 hearing on veterans benefits. Durbin has been a close adviser to his colleague from Illinois.

## Entering the Race

On February 10, 2007, as many as 15,000 people assembled outside the Old State Capitol in Springfield, Illinois, to hear Barack Obama officially announce his candidacy for president of the United States. Obama introduced several of his major campaign themes: ending the war in Iraq and creating a new politics, one that is more inclusive, less partisan, and more hopeful. "We all made this journey for a reason," he said.

> It's humbling, but in my heart I know you didn't come here just for me, you came here because you believe in what this country can be. In the face of war, you believe there can be peace. In the face of despair, you believe there can be hope. In the face of a politics that's shut you out, that's told you to settle, that's divided us for too long, you believe we can be one people, reaching for what's possible, building the more perfect union.

Barack Obama waves to supporters as he announces his candidacy for president of the United States, Springfield, Illinois, February 10, 2007.

Obama's words were, as usual, eloquent and inspiring. But at this point, almost two years before the presidential election, political experts gave him little chance of winning. To secure the Democratic Party's nomination for president, Obama would have to defeat a half dozen other candidates with impressive national credentials. None loomed larger than Senator Hillary Rodham Clinton of New York.

## The Front-runner

Hillary Clinton seemed to enjoy insurmountable advantages in the 2008 Democratic presidential primary race. She was familiar to, and widely respected by, Democratic voters across the country. She had been in the Senate since 2001. Before that, from 1993 to 2000, she was America's first lady. Her husband, former president Bill Clinton, remained immensely popular among Democrats. She had the support of the Democratic Party establishment and could raise huge amounts of money for her campaign.

To gain the Democratic nomination in 2008, a candidate would need to secure a total of 2,118 delegates, out of a total of 4,050. Most of the delegates would be allotted based on the results of voting in the state primary elections and caucuses. But there were almost 800 superdelegates; these were Democratic Party leaders who could vote for whomever they wished, regardless of the preferences of rank-and-file Democratic voters.

Hillary Clinton's campaign was based on a strategy of "inevitability." Most of the superdelegates favored her. She would

collect the lion's share of campaign contributions from wealthy Democratic donors. After she won the early primary contests, even Democrats who initially supported someone else would recognize that she was going to win the nomination. To give her the best chance of beating the Republican nominee in November, Democrats would rally around her early on.

## Upsets

Barack Obama had a different strategy. Quietly, he was taking the steps necessary

Early on, political analysts considered Senator Hillary Clinton the overwhelming favorite to win the Democratic Party's 2008 nomination for president.

to wage a long primary battle. Obama's campaign set up offices in state after state and focused on building grassroots support. It also found effective ways to use the Internet, collecting millions of dollars in small online donations and using social-networking sites to identify and mobilize volunteers.

Throughout 2007, however, political analysts continued to view Hillary Clinton as the overwhelming favorite to become the Democratic nominee. However, in the first contest—the Iowa caucuses, held on January 3, 2008—Barack Obama scored a stunning upset. He placed first, attracting 38 percent of the vote. Clinton finished third, with 29 percent.

It suddenly appeared that Obama, not Clinton, might lock up the nomination early. Political pundits suggested that if he won convincingly in the next contest, the New Hampshire primary, Clinton's campaign would be doomed. But on January 8, Clinton scored her own upset, winning New Hampshire by a 3 percent margin.

## Winning the Nomination

It had been widely expected that Hillary Clinton would lock up the Democratic nomination on February 5—dubbed Super Tuesday because 23 primary contests were scheduled for that day. But Obama won 13 of the contests. Over the next four weeks, he reeled off 11 consecutive victories, sending the Clinton campaign into a tailspin from which it would never completely recover. As Obama increased his lead in the number of pledged delegates (those won in primaries and caucuses), the unelected superdelegates began to move his way.

Obama did have his share of stumbles. In April, for example, he was trying to explain why Clinton consistently outpolled him among small-town, working-class voters. He commented that in economically difficult times, some people become bitter and "cling to guns or religion or antipathy to people who aren't like them." Clinton and Senator John McCain—who had by this time sewn up the Republican presidential nomination—were quick to cite this as evidence of Obama's arrogance and elitism. A few days after the remarks became public, Clinton beat Obama in Pennsylvania—a large "swing state" that might decide whether a Democrat or Republican won the general election.

But Obama managed to put the "bitter" controversy—like the controversy over his relationship with Reverend Wright—behind him. He erased the delegate gains Clinton had made in Pennsylvania by scoring a big victory in North Carolina on May 6.

It was clear that Clinton couldn't catch Obama in the delegate count. But she remained in the race until the last primary contests, on June 3. Obama finished with 2,229.5 delegates, more than enough to claim the nomination.

On August 23 Obama introduced his vice presidential running mate: longtime U.S. senator Joe Biden of Delaware. Five

Obama with his vice presidential running mate, Joe Biden of Delaware, at a rally in Toldedo, Ohio, August 31, 2008.

days later, at the Democratic National Convention in Denver, Obama accepted his party's nomination for president.

Polls taken right after the convention showed Obama leading McCain by 5 to 8 percentage points among voters nationwide. But in the United States, presidents aren't elected by the nation-wide popular vote. Instead, they must win a majority of votes in the electoral college.

## Obama vs. McCain

John McCain, the Republican presidential nominee, chose as his running mate a newcomer to national politics: Sarah Palin,

**READ MORE**

To find out how the electoral college works, see page 52.

the governor of Alaska. The choice pleased conservative Republicans and initially intrigued independent voters. Palin was said to be a tough-minded reformer. After the Republican National Convention in the first week of September, polls showed McCain with a small lead over Obama.

But questions began to emerge about Palin's record as Alaska governor and, more important, about her readiness to assume the presidency should McCain die or become incapacitated while in office. Palin seemed unfamiliar with even basic issues of policy and governance. Americans began to question McCain's judgment in selecting her.

Obama's poll numbers rebounded. McCain and his supporters pounded away at the Democratic nominee's inexperience, but when a financial crisis struck the country in late September, Obama appeared calmer, steadier, and better informed about the issues than did McCain. On September

**READ MORE**

To learn about John McCain, the 2008 Republican nominee for president, turn to page 53.

27, more than 50 million Americans watched the first presidential debate on TV, and Obama was judged the clear winner. The majority of viewers said Obama won the two succeeding debates as well. Though relatively new to national politics, Obama appeared ready to be president.

Throughout October, Obama continued to hold a significant lead in national opinion polls. More important, state-by-state polls showed him ahead in the race for electoral votes. Obama led in most of the swing states, and he was competitive in states that Republicans normally took for granted, such as Indiana, Virginia, and North Carolina. Obama's calm, steady demeanor and his dedication to maintaining a civil tone in political discussion—even in the face of highly personal Republican attacks—reassured voters. America seemed to be buying into Obama's vision of a better politics.

## Historic Vote

On November 4, Americans went to the polls to choose the 44th president of the United States. Turnout was huge, with more than 126 million people casting ballots. That was the highest total ever. And the voters made a momentous choice: for the first time in U.S. history, an African American was elected to the

Barack Obama, 44th president of the United States, on the night of his election. Hundreds of thousands of people crowded into Chicago's Grant Park to hear Obama's victory speech (opposite page).

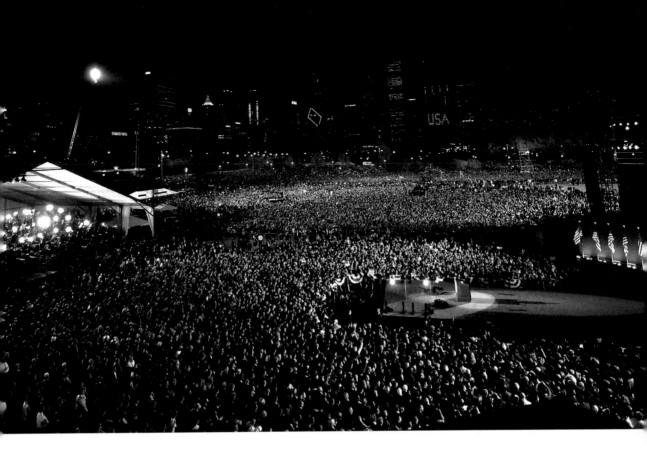

nation's highest office. Barack Obama won a solid majority of the popular vote, about 52 percent to John McCain's 46 percent. Obama won a landslide in the electoral college, garnering 365 electoral votes.

The historic significance of the election could hardly be missed. "And so it came to pass," wrote Thomas Friedman in the *New York Times*, "that on Nov. 4, 2008, . . . the American Civil War ended." The nation's age-old racial wounds, it seemed, might finally heal.

At a massive election-night victory rally in Chicago's Grant Park, the president-elect assessed how far the nation had come, but focused on the work still to be done. "That is the true genius of America—that America can change," Obama said. "Our union can be perfected. And what we have already achieved gives us hope for what we can and must achieve tomorrow."

# CROSS-CURRENTS

## Race in America: A Troubled Legacy

The United States Constitution was drafted in 1787, by American leaders who wanted to create a just and lasting form of government. To an extraordinary degree, they succeeded. The government of the United States has survived, and enabled the nation to flourish, for more than 220 years.

But the framers of the Constitution failed to resolve an important issue. Although one of the Constitution's stated purposes was "to secure the Blessings of Liberty" for the American people, the framers permitted slavery to continue. America's black slaves were finally freed as a result of the Civil War (1861–1865).

Yet in many parts of the country, African Americans continued to suffer mistreatment. In the South, a system of laws and practices known as Jim Crow kept blacks and whites segregated, or separated. Under this arrangement, blacks were inevitably treated as inferior. The civil rights movement of the 1950s and 1960s would help end Jim Crow. Legislation was passed that guaranteed African Americans equal treatment under the law.

Still, that didn't guarantee actual equality. Blacks had been discriminated against for centuries, and it was unreasonable to expect that the awful legacy of

Jim Crow era: An African American child in the South at a water fountain for "colored" people, 1938.

racism would immediately disappear. So in the mid-1960s, the government began a policy known as affirmative action. It sought to "level the playing field" so that black people received their share of educational and job opportunities. Affirmative action was seen as a temporary measure. The policy should be maintained, supporters said, only until social conditions for black Americans were on a par with social conditions for white Americans. Then blacks and whites could compete for jobs, college scholarships, and the like on an equal basis.

Many white people grew resentful as affirmative action was implemented, however. They complained of being denied admission to the college of their choice, or being passed over for a job they wanted, in favor of black candidates who were less qualified. Critics called affirmative action "reverse discrimination." They said it wasn't fair to punish whites for past injustices they personally had nothing to do with.

These kinds of grievances continue today. Many blacks have noted that American society still disadvantages them in significant ways. Some whites counter that African Americans want to play the role of victims to gain special advantages. Race remains a controversial issue in American life.

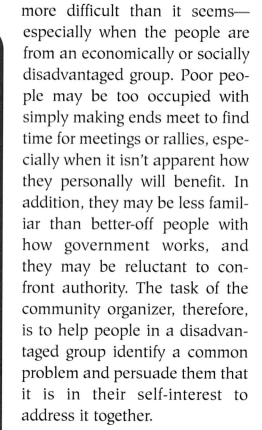

# CROSS-CURRENTS

## The How and Why of Community Organizing

Community organizing is a method of promoting social change. It seeks to empower ordinary people to improve their own lives by joining with others who share the same problems and demanding action from public officials.

A government agency or official will find it relatively easy to ignore the concerns of individuals. When many people act together, however, it is much more difficult to ignore them. Unity creates power, and officials tend to respond to power.

But unifying people around a common problem is often more difficult than it seems—especially when the people are from an economically or socially disadvantaged group. Poor people may be too occupied with simply making ends meet to find time for meetings or rallies, especially when it isn't apparent how they personally will benefit. In addition, they may be less familiar than better-off people with how government works, and they may be reluctant to confront authority. The task of the community organizer, therefore, is to help people in a disadvantaged group identify a common problem and persuade them that it is in their self-interest to address it together.

Saul Alinsky, 1968.

# The Father of Community Organizing

When Barack Obama went to work for the Calumet Community Religious Conference, the people who taught him about community organizing were all schooled in a model of action devised by Saul Alinsky (1909–1972). Alinsky is considered the father of modern community organizing. At the heart of his method was "agitation." The organizer, Alinsky said, should "rub raw the sores of discontent," making people angry enough about the rotten state of their lives to take action.

During the 1930s, after receiving a degree in criminology from the University of Chicago, Alinsky worked with residents of Chicago's rough Back of the Yards neighborhood. By setting up a neighborhood council, he helped reduce ethnic tensions there, then got residents to focus their anger on the terrible working conditions at the Back of the Yards' meatpacking plants. Eventually, the plant owners gave in to some of the workers' demands.

Alinsky went on to launch organizing campaigns all over the country. He also wrote extensively about his ideas and methods. He believed that people in power would never help the underprivileged simply because that was the right thing to do. They had to be forced to do so, through tactics such as confrontation and ridicule.

Barack Obama, according to his mentor Gerald Kellman, never fully embraced this aspect of Saul Alinsky's teaching. "Barack did not like direct confrontation. . . . He was more comfortable in dialogue with people," Kellman told a reporter.

# Bobby Rush vs. Barack Obama

Barack Obama had been in the Illinois state senate for only three years when he decided to run for a seat in the U.S. House of Representatives. Obama mounted a 2000 primary challenge against Bobby Rush in the First Congressional District of Illinois. The First District included the South Side of Chicago.

Born in Georgia in 1946, Rush had moved with his family to Chicago as a child. He served in the military between 1963 and 1968. He then went on to cofound the Illinois chapter of the Black Panthers, an organization devoted to defending the rights of African Americans—by force if necessary. Rush worked as a community activist and served on Chicago's City Council before being elected in 1992, to his first term in Congress. He won reelection in 1994, 1996, and 1998. But in 1999, Rush ran in the Democratic primary for Chicago mayor. He was beaten badly by the incumbent mayor, Richard M. Daley, and did poorly among African Americans, even though Daley is white.

Congressman Bobby Rush.

Because of this, Barack Obama believed Rush might be politically vulnerable in his own district, which was largely black.

Obama's hallmarks as a state senator had been his civil, nonconfrontational style and his cerebral approach to the issues. But the race against Rush became very personal. With his Harvard Law degree and his professorial manner of speaking, Obama was accused of being arrogant. He hadn't grown up on the South Side, and he came from middle-class roots, so he was painted as an outsider who was out of touch with the low-income residents of the First District. That charge was reinforced by the Obamas' residence in the upscale Hyde Park neighborhood. The ugliest attacks, however, involved race. Rush supporters questioned whether Obama was "black enough." Donne Trotter, an African American state senator, put it more bluntly. "Barack is viewed in part to be the white man in blackface in our community," Trotter said.

Obama's attempts to stay above the fray, longtime Chicago political observers said, didn't help him. Many of the charges seemed to stick.

In March 2000, when the Democratic primary was held, Rush beat Obama convincingly. The incumbent received 60 percent of the vote to Obama's 30 percent.

# CROSS-CURRENTS

# The Electoral College

In the United States, presidential candidates do not win office simply by getting more votes nationwide than their opponents. Instead, they must win a majority of votes in the electoral college.

When Americans cast their votes for president, they are also choosing representatives (or electors) to serve in the electoral college. Later, these electors meet and essentially validate the results of the presidential election. Under this system, each state is allotted a number of votes in the electoral college equal to that state's representation in Congress. There are 535 members of Congress. Each of the 50 states has two U.S. senators, for a total of 100. The House of Representatives has 435 seats, which are apportioned by state population (each state has at least one seat, and larger states have more seats).

Thus, in presidential elections, each state has at least 3 electoral votes; California, the state with the largest population, has 55 electoral votes. Even though it is not represented in the U.S. Senate, Washington, D.C., is allotted 3 electoral votes, bringing the total number of electoral votes to 538.

To win the presidency, a candidate must receive a majority of votes in the electoral college (at least 270). Except in the cases of Maine and Nebraska, the candidate who wins the popular vote in a state wins all its electoral votes. Thus it is possible for a candidate to receive more votes nationwide but still not win the election (which happened in 2000).

# John McCain

John McCain, the 2008 Republican nominee for president, first won fame as a war hero. The son and grandson of American admirals, McCain was himself a U.S. Navy pilot. In 1967, during the Vietnam War, McCain was flying a mission over North Vietnam when his plane was hit by a surface-to-air missile. He ejected from the plane and parachuted to the ground but sustained serious injuries.

McCain was captured and tortured. When the North Vietnamese learned that he was the son of an admiral, they offered to release him. McCain refused, because the military code of honor required that prisoners of war be released in the order in which they were captured. McCain, along with other American POWs, was finally released in March 1973.

McCain retired from the navy in 1981. The following year, he won a seat in the U.S. House of Representatives from Arizona's First Congressional District. He was elected to the U.S. Senate in 1985. McCain won a fourth term in 2004.

Though a Republican, McCain gained a reputation for independence. In the Senate, he often opposed his party's leadership and worked with Democrats.

In 2000 McCain made a bid for the Republican presidential nomination. He ultimately lost to George W. Bush.

John McCain, longtime U.S. senator from Arizona, was the Republican nominee for president in 2008.

# Chronology

**1961:** Barack Obama is born in Honolulu, Hawaii, on August 4.

**1967:** Moves to Indonesia with his mother and stepfather.

**1971:** Returns to Hawaii to live with grandparents. Enrolls in prestigious Punahou School as a fifth grader.

**1979:** Graduates from Punahou. Enrolls in Occidental College in Los Angeles.

**1981:** Transfers to Columbia University in New York.

**1983:** Graduates from Columbia with a degree in political science.

**1985:** Accepts a job as a community organizer in Chicago.

**1988:** Enters Harvard Law School.

**1990:** Elected the first African American president of the *Harvard Law Review*.

**1991:** Graduates with honors from Harvard.

**1992:** Marries Michelle Robinson on October 3.

**1993:** Accepts position at Chicago firm specializing in civil rights law. Begins teaching at the University of Chicago Law School.

**1995:** Publishes his memoir, *Dreams from My Father: A Story of Race and Inheritance*.

**1996:** Obama wins election to the Illinois state senate.

**1998:** Daughter Malia is born.

**2000:** Loses primary race for a seat in the U.S. House of Representatives.

**2001:** Daughter Sasha is born.

**2002:** Makes speech in Chicago opposing the Bush administration's plans to invade Iraq.

**2004:** Delivers keynote address at the Democratic National Convention in Boston on July 27. Is elected to the U.S. Senate.

**2005:** Sworn in as a U.S. senator in January.

**2006:** Second book, *The Audacity of Hope*, is published.

**2007:** On February 10, announces his candidacy for the presidency of the United States.

**2008:** Wins Democratic nomination after long primary campaign against Hillary Clinton. Selects Senator Joe Biden as vice presidential running mate. On November 4, is elected 44th president of the United States in a convincing victory over Republican John McCain.

**2009:** On January 20, a huge crowd comes to Washington, D.C., to witness the historic inauguration of Barack Obama. In February, President Obama signs a $787 billion economic stimulus package into law.

# Further Reading

Davis, William Michael. *Barack Obama: The Politics of Hope.* Stockton, N.J.: OTTN Publishing, 2008.

Dupuis, Martin, and Keith Boeckelman. *Barack Obama, The New Face of American Politics.* Westport, Conn.: Praeger Publishers, 2008.

Obama, Barack. *Dreams from My Father: A Story of Race and Inheritance.* Rev ed. New York: Three Rivers Press, 2004.

Wilson, John K. *Barack Obama: This Improbable Quest.* Boulder, Colo.: Paradigm Publishers, 2008.

# Internet Resources

**http://www.barackobama.com**

> Barack Obama's official 2008 presidential campaign Web site includes a biography, transcripts of speeches, news updates, and more.

**http://www.reuters.com/news/globalcoverage/barackobama**

> Hosted by Reuters, this site contains news on all aspects of the 2008 presidential campaign.

**http://www.Projects.washingtonpost.com/ 2008-presidential-candidates/barack-obama**

> Hosted by *The Washington Post,* this site offers collected news and analysis of the presidential candidates.

# Glossary

**bill**—proposed legislation under consideration by a legislative body.

**caucus**—a formal gathering of political party members who vote for political candidates.

**delegate**—in a presidential campaign, a person elected by voters to attend a political party's national convention and vote for a given candidate.

**grassroots**—basic or fundamental; originating with or involving ordinary people rather than leaders.

**legacy**—something received from the past.

**partisan**—making decisions based on the political party one belongs to.

**primary**—a preliminary election in which voters of each political party nominate candidates for office.

# Chapter Notes

p. 9: "We the people . . ." Remarks of Senator Barack Obama: "A More Perfect Union," Philadelphia, PA, March 18, 2008. http://www.barackobama.com/2008/03/18/remarks_of_senator_barack_obam_53.php

p. 9: "to continue the long march . . ." Ibid.

p. 10: "I can no more . . ." Ibid.

p. 10: "firm conviction—a conviction . . ." Ibid.

p. 12: "Let us find . . ." Ibid.

p. 12: "After running a campaign . . ." Jeff Zeleny, "Obama Urges U.S. to Grapple with Race Issue," *New York Times*, March 19, 2008. http://www.nytimes.com/2008/03/19/us/politics/19obama.html?pagewanted=print

p. 12: "about slavery, black anger . . ." Liz Halloran, "Obama's Race Speech Heralded as Historic," www.usnews.com, March 18, 2008. http://www.usnews.com/articles/news/campaign-2008/2008/03/18/obamas-race-speech-heralded-as-historic.html

p. 15: "one long adventure . . ." Barack Obama, *Dreams From My Father: A Story of Race and Inheritance*, rev. ed. (New York: Three Rivers Press, 2004), 37.

p. 17: "biggest struggles were . . ." Kirsten Scharnberg and Kim Barker, "The Not-So-Simple Story of Barack Obama's Youth," *Chicago Tribune*, March 25, 2007. http://www.chicagotribune.com/news/politics/chi-0703250359mar25,0,7910127.story

p. 18: "I was engaged . . ." Ibid., 76.

p. 18: "Clearly the guy had . . ." Larry Gordon, "Occidental Recalls 'Barry' Obama," *Los Angeles Times*, January 27, 2007.

p. 18: "My identity might . . ." Obama, *Dreams*, 111.

p. 21: "felt pangs of guilt . . ." Obama, *Dreams*, 136.

p. 22: "The guy was just . . ." Bob Secter and John McCormick, "Portrait of a Pragmatist," *Chicago Tribune*, March 9, 2007.

p. 22: "He was ambitious . . ." David Mendell, *Obama: From Promise to Power* (New York: Amistad, 2007), 72.

p. 25: "I just can't . . ." Ibid., 82.

p. 25: "A lot of people . . ." Michael Levenson and Jonathan Saltzman, "At Harvard Law, a Unifying Voice," *Boston Globe*, January 28, 2007.

p. 26: "one of the two most talented . . ." Garrett M. Graff, "The Legend of Barack Obama," Washingtonian.com, November 1. 2006. http://www.washingtonian.com/print/articles/6/174/1836.html

p. 27: "Whatever his politics . . ." Jodi Kantor, "In Law School, Obama Found Political Voice," *New York Times*, January 28, 2007. http://www.nytimes.com/2007/01/28/us/politics/28obama.html?pagewanted=all

p. 27: "This bridge-building . . ." Mendell, *Obama*, 85.

p. 29: "People are hungry . . ." Ibid., 112.

p. 30: "He is idealistic . . ." Ibid., 128.

p. 33: "based not on reason . . ." BarackObama.com, Remarks of Illinois State Sen. Barack Obama Against Going to War with Iraq, October 2, 2002. http://www.barackobama.com/2002/10/02/remarks_of_illinois_state_sen.php

p. 34: "I am not running . . ." Mendell, *Obama*, 188.

p. 34: "We have shared values . . ." William Finnegan, "The Candidate," *New Yorker*, May 31, 2004. http://www.newyorker.com/archive/2004/05/31/040531fa_fact1

p. 36: "I'm feeling very much . . ." Jonathan Alter, "The Audacity of Hope," *Newsweek*, January 3, 2005.

p. 38: "We all made this journey . . ." BarackObama.com, Full Text of Senator Barack Obama's Announcement for President, February 10, 2007. http://www.barackobama.com/2007/02/10/remarks_of_senator_barack_obam_11.php

p. 41: "cling to guns . . ." "Rivals Pounce on Obama's 'Bitter' Remarks," CBS News, April 12, 2008. http://www.cbsnews.com/stories/2008/04/12/politics/main4011339.shtml

p. 45: "And so it came to pass . . ." Thomas L. Friedman, "Finishing Our Work," *New York Times*, November 5, 2008.

p. 45: "That is the true genius . . ." Text of Barack Obama's acceptance speech, November 4, 2008. http://news.bbc.co.uk/2/hi/americas/us_elections_2008/7710038.stm

p. 49: "rub raw the sores . . ." "A Time for Pride," *Time*, May 22, 1964. http://www.time.com/time/magazine/article/0,9171,871153,00.html

p. 49: "Barack did not like . . ." David Moberg, "Obama's Community Roots," *The Nation* (April 16, 2007), p. 18.

p. 51: "Barack is viewed in part . . ." Michael Weisskopf, "Obama: How He Learned to Win," *Time* (May 8, 2008). http://www.time.com/time/magazine/article/0,9171,1738494,00.html

# Index

Numbers in **bold italics** refer to captions.

# Photo Credits

# About the Author

CAMMY S. BOURCIER is a writer and television producer who has worked on a wide range of projects—from pharmaceutical breakthroughs to Holocaust discoveries. She wrote "Shadows of the 70s," a 65-part series recapping that decade for the Associated Press, and has had more than 500 articles published on food trends.